>> CODE POWER: A TEEN PROGRAMMER'S GUIDE™

GETTING TO KNOW
the Raspberry Pi

NICKI PETER PETRIKOWSKI

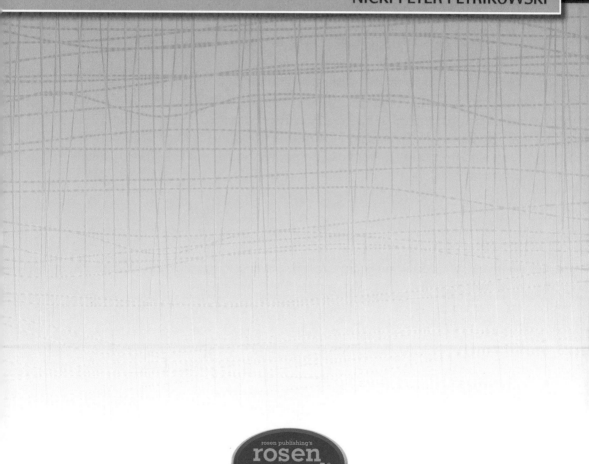

rosen publishing's
rosen
central®

NEW YORK

Published in 2015 by The Rosen Publishing Group, Inc.
29 East 21st Street, New York, NY 10010

Library of Congress Cataloging-in-Publication Data

Petrikowski, Nicki Peter, author.
Getting to know the Raspberry Pi / Nicki Peter Petrikowski. — First edition.
     pages cm. — (Code power: a teen programmer's guide)
Audience: Grades 5-8.
Includes bibliographical references and index.
ISBN 978-1-4777-7709-1 (library bound) — ISBN 978-1-4777-7711-4 (pbk.) — ISBN 978-1-4777-7712-1 (6-pack)
1. Raspberry Pi (Computer)—Juvenile literature. 2. Pocket computers—Juvenile literature. 3. Python (Computer program language—Juvenile literature. I. Title.
QA76.8.R15P48 2015
004.1675—dc23

                                                        2013044305

Manufactured in the United States of America

{CONTENTS

{INTROD

I t sounds delicious, and many people would agree that it is. The Raspberry Pi is a very affordable minicomputer that is only about the size of a credit card. It has taken the world of computing by storm since it was released in early 2012.

The Raspberry Pi was originally envisioned as a device to be produced in small numbers. It was intended to be used in schools to get students interested in working with computers and programming, with the goal of having more people study computer science at college. Its immense success surprised even the creators of the tiny computer, who expected to sell maybe ten thousand of their boards. Instead, more than one million Raspberry Pis were sold within little more than a year of its initial release—and not just to schools.

The flexible, low-cost computer can do most things other computers can: You can use it to write a letter, surf the Internet, watch videos, and play games. Beyond that, the open nature of the Raspberry Pi has inspired people of all ages around the globe to experiment with programming and electronics. People have come up with countless creative projects using

UCTION

The Raspberry Pi presents a lot of possibilities in a neat little package.

the device, from building a cheap media center or an arcade machine to a small supercomputer. There are projects that plan to use the Raspberry Pi to explore the ocean and even space. The combination of the Raspberry Pi's low price, small size, and low power consumption opens up many possibilities.

In the following pages, you will learn about the vision behind the Raspberry Pi and the history of its creation, the hardware it uses, and the options it offers in terms of operating systems, software, and programming languages. You will also get a look at the lively Raspberry Pi community of hackers and tinkerers and the variety of exciting ideas that they have come up with to make use of the minicomputer.

It may seem daunting at first, but programming and physical computing…it's as easy as Pi!

RASPBERRY PI HISTORY: FROM ITS CONCEPTION TO THE PRESENT DAY

T he British science fiction writer Arthur C. Clarke noted in what is known as his Third Law that any sufficiently advanced technology is indistinguishable from magic. You don't have to venture into the realm of science fiction to see that there is truth to this: for many people today, computers work as if by magic. They may know what buttons to push, which keys to press, and which icons to click to get the desired result, but how the computer works remains a mystery to them. Giving people, especially children and youths, a tool to further their understanding of how computers work was the goal that led to the creation of the Raspberry Pi.

INCEPTION OF A REVOLUTIONARY COMPUTER

Eben Upton, along with some of his colleagues, had the idea for a small and inexpensive computer for young people in 2006,

Eben Upton, seen here holding a prototype of the Raspberry Pi, has made a big impact on the computing world with his small creation.

when he was the director of studies in computer science at Cambridge University in England. He noticed that many of the students coming to study computer science did not have any real experience with programming, which had been natural for earlier generations wanting to work in this field.

When computers first found their way into family homes in the 1980s in the form of the Commodore 64, the ZX Spectrum, or the Atari ST, they were far from the user-friendly machines we know today. To get these machines to do what you wanted, you had to put in some effort and have at least a basic understanding of how computers and programming worked. Since users were forced to take the first step, the second step came easier, and a lot of people were sent on their way to deeper knowledge about computing. Many who went on to work in the computer industry taught themselves to program on these early home computers. As the ease of use increased over the years with preinstalled operating systems and graphical user interfaces, people were no longer forced to educate themselves about how a computer works. Many spared themselves the effort and became passive users without any real computer knowledge.

Similarly, the information and technology classes in schools, which were often the only formal preparation for young people applying to study computer science at college, focused on how to use office software and do a bit of Web page design. Those are certainly not bad skills to have, but they were insufficient from a computer scientist's point of view. Hence Eben Upton, who had in the meantime gone on to work as a chip architect for Broadcom, a big company producing integrated circuits for computer and telecommunication networking, set out to create

Legendary computer programmer David Braben is one of the supporters of the Raspberry Pi project. His goal is to get more young people to learn to code.

a small computer that was cheap enough for everyone to afford. He wanted something that students could use for experimenting, without the fear of damaging or breaking a device costing hundreds of dollars. To this end, in November 2008, he formed the Raspberry Pi Foundation, a United Kingdom registered charity with the goal of furthering the education of children and adults, particularly in the field of computer science.

Other leaders of the project—and trustees of the foundation—included Dr. Rob Mullins and Professor Alan Mycroft, colleagues of Upton's from the computer lab at Cambridge University; Jack Lang, a lecturer in entrepreneurship at the university; and Pete Lomas, managing director at Norcott Technologies, a hardware design and production company. The team also included David Braben, a programmer best known for cocreating *Elite*, a video game about trading and fighting in space first released in 1984. The game was immensely popular during the heyday of the aforementioned early home computers, and it influenced many games that came after it.

At Broadcom, Eben Upton experienced firsthand the evolution of the hardware used in high-end cell phones: microchips that were small but had increasingly high capabilities. They were fairly inexpensive, at least when bought in larger quantities. Using this hardware, Upton created several prototypes of his envisioned minicomputer that changed considerably over the years.

In May 2011, there came a turning point for the Raspberry Pi, when tech journalist Rory Cellan-Jones from the British Broadcasting Corporation (BBC) put a video of the prototype on his blog. It went viral, with six hundred thousand views in only

>> THE RASPBERRY PI COMMUNITY

In the *Raspberry Pi User Guide*, Eben Upton notes on behalf of the Raspberry Pi Foundation, "The Raspberry Pi community is one of the things we're proudest of." After the success of the video made by Rory Cellan-Jones in May 2011, the wide interest became apparent and the foundation opened a forum on its website (http://www.raspberrypi.org). This forum now has over sixty thousand members discussing all things Raspberry Pi, from troubleshooting for beginners

Working with minicomputers has become a hobby for many. Gatherings of Pi enthusiasts, called Raspberry Jams, take place all over the world.

to complex programming projects. Additionally, fan sites can be found on the Internet by the hundreds, with new ones being created every day. Still, the foundation's own website with its daily updated blog remains the cornerstone of the community.

Fans of the Raspberry Pi gather not only in the digital arena, but also in the physical world. Monthly meetings commonly known as Raspberry Jams—the community seems to appreciate puns— allow for enthusiasts to exchange ideas and present projects. Raspberry Jams take place all over the world. To see if there is one near you, check the event calendar on the network's website (http:// raspberryjam.org.uk).

The first issue of a monthly fanzine, *The MagPi*, which offers articles, project guides, and tutorials for the Raspberry Pi, was made available free for download in May 2012, when many people were still eagerly awaiting the arrival of their Raspberry Pi. This fanzine proved to be so popular that it managed to raise almost $45,000 on Kickstarter in December 2012, five times the funding goal, to make it available as a printed magazine in addition to its digital form.

two days. Apparently a lot of people were interested in a small computer like this, especially since Upton had said the cost of the final product would be about the same as a textbook, or about $25. The next months were spent adjusting the prototype with this price point in mind, trying to keep costs down while keeping the usability and the features the same.

For testing and demonstrations, fifty alpha boards were produced in August 2011. These were larger than the planned final product but functionally identical. Twenty-five beta boards that had the same layout as the version intended for mass production followed in December. In January 2012, the Raspberry Pi Foundation auctioned off the beta boards with serial numbers 1 to 10 on eBay. The organization raised over $24,000, roughly seven hundred times the retail price of ten Model B Raspberry Pi boards, a testament to the extraordinary interest in the minicomputer. The money raised went toward the foundation's charity work. An anonymous buyer donated Board #7 to the Centre for Computing History, a computer museum in Haverhill, England. The donor apparently was confident that the Raspberry Pi would leave its mark on history. The following success story proved him right.

UNEXPECTED SUCCESS: THE RASPBERRY PI HITS THE MARKET

The general release of the Raspberry Pi was planned for February 2012 with ten thousand units, but it soon became apparent that demand was much higher. Ten times higher, in fact, because the Raspberry Pi Foundation already had one hundred thousand people on its mailing list waiting for the chance to buy their own minicomputers. Hence, the decision was made not to produce the Raspberry Pi in-house—or in Jack Lang's garage, as was originally planned—but to outsource it to Premier Farnell/Element 14 and RS Components, two microelectronics suppliers based in the United Kingdom. They had the infrastructure in place to produce the Raspberry Pi in larger numbers.

Demand was so high that the websites of both companies crashed for large parts of February 29, 2012, the day of release.

In fact, the demand was so great that sales had to be limited to one Raspberry Pi per customer. (This order limit has since been lifted.) Within three months more than half a million units were sold, although customers often had to wait for months to receive their order; production could not keep up with the demand. In February 2013, to make the minicomputer more easily available in China, the Raspberry Pi Foundation granted EGOMAN Technology Corporation a license to produce and distribute Raspberry Pis. These units have a red board, rather than the green board of those produced in England. The milestone of one million units sold worldwide was reached in early 2013. By late October of the same year, a second million were sold, with no sign of the success abating anytime soon.

RASPBERRY PI RECIPE: HARDWARE INGREDIENTS

W hat does it take to make a Raspberry Pi? That depends, since there are two different versions available: Model A and Model B.

The most obvious difference between the two versions is the price: Model A costs $25, while Model B costs $35. The difference in price is because Model B has 512MB RAM, two USB ports, and a 10/100 Ethernet controller, whereas Model A has only 256MB RAM, one USB port, and no built-in Ethernet controller. That not only makes Model A cheaper, but it also means that it has lower power consumption, which can be an important factor depending on what you intend to do with the Raspberry Pi. Generally speaking, though, the advantages of Model B are well worth the extra $10. The cost savings of Model A only make a real difference for schools or other organizations looking to buy the Raspberry Pi in larger numbers.

Aside from these differences, Model A and Model B are the same. The heart of both models of the Raspberry Pi is the Broadcom BCM2835, which is a so-called system-on-chip (SoC).

Most computers use several individual chips, such as a central processing unit (CPU) and a graphics processing unit (GPU). However, a system-on-chip, as the name suggests, integrates the majority of the system's components into one chip. SoCs are common in small mobile devices like cell phones because they use relatively little power. The SoC built into the Raspberry Pi includes an ARM1176JZF-S 700 MHz processor and a Videocore 4 GPU. Since the SoC in the Raspberry Pi uses a different chip architecture, called ARM, than that used for the chips in most regular personal computers, called x86, most software written with the x86 architecture in mind will not run on the Raspberry Pi.

Both models feature an SD card reader, two different video outputs (HDMI and composite video), a 3.5 mm audio output, a micro USB power port, and a 26-pin GPIO port. GPIO stands for general-purpose input/output. The GPIO sets the Raspberry Pi apart from many other computers because external hardware such as sensors and servos can be connected to it, and it can be used as a controller for an electronic circuit (to turn LEDs on and off, for example).

GETTING THE RASPBERRY PI TO WORK: NECESSARY PERIPHERALS

The board on its own is not functional. There are some things required to make it usable. First you need a 5-volt micro USB power charger, which is the same kind many cell phones use, because without power the Raspberry Pi can't run. The board does not have an on/off switch. To switch it on, you simply power it up; to switch it off, you remove power. Therefore, you should connect all the peripherals before plugging in the power supply. You need a monitor or a TV that you can connect to one of the Pi's video outputs and a cable to connect it with. You need a keyboard and a mouse as input devices that can be connected to the USB ports. If your peripherals don't have the right plugs, there may be adapters available to make them usable.

When all the peripherals are connected, the Raspberry Pi is ready to get to work.

Finally, you need an SD card. Unlike most other personal computers, the Raspberry Pi does not have a hard disk drive, so the SD card is used for storing data. The minimum size SD card that can be used with the Raspberry Pi is 2 gigabytes. However, since most of that will be needed for the operating system, which is installed on the SD card, a card with at least 4GB

is recommended. Cards of up to 32GB have been tried with the Raspberry Pi. Most cards seem to work, but if you want to be sure, there is information on which cards work best on the Raspberry Pi Foundation's website, http://www .raspberrypi.org. You may also need access to another computer equipped with a card reader to prepare the SD card, although there are SD cards available with the operating system preinstalled.

ENHANCING YOUR PI: USEFUL ACCESSORIES

Aside from these things that are absolutely necessary to work with the Raspberry Pi, there are other peripherals, which, while not strictly needed, can be useful. The first item is an external USB hub. The two USB ports on the Model B are usually used for a keyboard and a mouse, which means you can't connect anything else to it. A hub will take up one of the USB ports

>> A CASE FOR THE RASPBERRY PI

It is not strictly necessary to have a case for your Raspberry Pi, as it is safe to run it without one. Nonetheless, having a case to protect the computer from dust, accidentally spilled beverages, or damage from static electricity is a good idea.

While the producers of the Raspberry Pi currently do not offer a case themselves, there are cases available to buy from third-party manufacturers like ModMyPi (http://www.modmypi.com), PiHolder (http://www.piholder.com), and PiBow (http://shop.pimoroni.com). See-through cases seem particularly popular, so you can protect your board while still being able to look at it.

While the Raspberry Pi does not necessarily need a case, it's better to be safe than sorry. And building or customizing a case can be fun.

In keeping with the do-it-yourself spirit of the Raspberry Pi, many people choose to build their own case, either by modifying a box or tin of approximately the right size or by building one from scratch. Since the board does not produce a lot of heat and therefore does not need cooling unless the ambient temperature is extremely high, this is relatively easy. Probably the easiest way is to make one out of paper or cardboard. The template for such a case, known as a Punnet, can be downloaded from the website of the Raspberry Pi Foundation (http://www.raspberrypi.org/archives/1310). This template could also be helpful for building a case out of a sturdier material like wood. It helps you with the main difficulty: placing the openings correctly so that you have easy access to the computer's ports.

Another popular option for building a case that is in keeping with the Raspberry Pi's playful nature is to make one out of LEGOs. Old gaming consoles and cartridges have also been modified to serve as cases for the Raspberry Pi, which seems fitting if the device is intended to be used for retro gaming.

Many users of the Raspberry Pi like to let their imaginations run wild with their projects for a case, as well as for the computer itself.

on the board, but in turn, it offers more USB ports for plugging in items like a USB stick or an external hard drive, giving you a lot more options. A powered USB hub is recommended, as the 5-volt power charger does not provide enough power for other peripherals to run reliably.

Other things that can be useful depending on the intended purpose of the Raspberry Pi would be an Ethernet cable, if you want to connect to a network or the Internet via a modem; a Wi-Fi

The optional camera module for the Raspberry Pi opens up many possibilities for interesting projects.

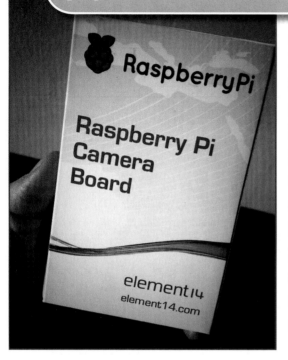

dongle, if you want to go wireless; or a Bluetooth adapter. Since May 2013, a camera module for the Raspberry Pi has been available. It can take high-quality pictures and make videos, but it does not record sound. If you do not use the HDMI port to connect a display to the Pi, you may want some speakers. A case for the minicomputer is also worth considering.

NOT SUITED TO EVERY TASK: ALTERNATIVES TO THE RASPBERRY PI

The intention of the Raspberry Pi Foundation was to make a computer cheap enough so that almost everyone could afford it. To that end, it was designed to use components that you might have lying around the house, like a cell phone charger or an old keyboard. Being able to use a TV as display, like the early home computers from the 1980s did, cuts costs considerably compared to a computer for which you have to buy a monitor. If, however, you do not have these items available and need to buy them in order to turn your Raspberry Pi board into a functioning system, costs could add up quickly. In this situation, it might be preferable to look for a cheap netbook or tablet computer, depending on the uses you have in mind.

Another thing to consider is the Raspberry Pi's computing power. In the FAQs on its website, the Raspberry Pi Foundation compares the performance of its board to that of a 300Mhz Pentium II, but with better graphics. The graphics are said to be roughly equivalent to those of the original Xbox and capable of Blu-ray quality playback. To put that into perspective, the Pentium II was top of the line in 1997, while the first Xbox was released in November 2001. Unlike a regular computer, it is not possible to upgrade the Raspberry Pi by adding more RAM. That means that if you want to run the latest programs and games, the Raspberry Pi is not your computer of choice, which would be a bit much to expect from a board for $25 or $35. However, the device is powerful enough to use for office work, retro gaming, hosting websites, running a media center, and countless creative projects, as well as its originally intended purpose of using it to learn how computers work and how to program them.

RASPBERRY PI PREPARATION: OS AND SOFTWARE

The majority of desktop and laptop computers use either Microsoft Windows or OS X as their operating system (OS). These operating systems do not work on the Raspberry Pi, though, because of its chip architecture. Instead, the Raspberry Pi usually uses a version of GNU/Linux as its OS.

CHOOSING AND INSTALLING AN OPERATING SYSTEM

The GNU Project, started in 1984, propagates free software. The idea of free software does not primarily have to do with the price, although many pieces of software developed with this philosophy in mind are indeed free in the sense that you don't have to pay for them. Foremost, "free" means that the software is open source. Unlike closed-source software like Windows, for which only Microsoft has access to the source code, anyone can download, study, and modify the source code of free software under the GNU General Public License.

Linux is a free operating system first created by Linus Torvalds, a Finnish computer science student, in 1991. It has since

Linus Torvalds created the Linux operating system, which is popular among Raspberry Pi users. A penguin named Tux is its official mascot.

been modified many times. The different versions of Linux are known as distributions, or distros. One of the most popular operating systems for the Raspberry Pi is a version of the Linux distro Debian. It has been optimized for use with the minicomputer and has therefore been named Raspbian. It can be downloaded from its own dedicated website (http://www.raspbian.org) or from the website of the Raspberry Pi Foundation, where other operating systems that work well on the minicomputer are also available.

To download your OS of choice and to install it on your SD card, you need access to another computer, although some vendors offer preprogrammed SD cards, which allow you to circumvent this step.

To make it usable, the operating system needs to be flashed to the SD card, which is a bit more complicated than simply copying the file onto the card. You need a tool called Win32DiskImager if the computer you use for the process runs Windows or a utility called dd if the computer uses Linux or OS X. An extensive guide on how to flash the image of your chosen operating system to an SD card can be found at http://elinux.org/RPi_Easy_SD_Card_Setup. Note that the previous contents of the SD card getting flashed are erased completely. If you want to flash a card that has been used before,

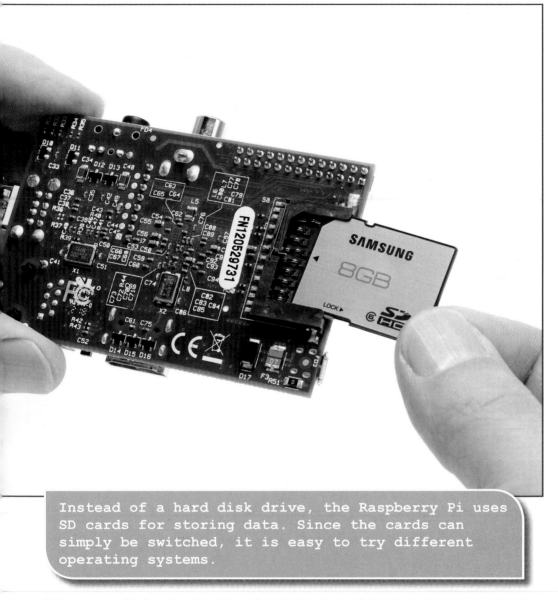

Instead of a hard disk drive, the Raspberry Pi uses SD cards for storing data. Since the cards can simply be switched, it is easy to try different operating systems.

it is a good idea to double-check that no data is going to be lost that you do not want to be deleted.

If you want to try another OS on your Raspberry Pi, you can simply reflash your SD card, or you can use different cards with

>> OPERATING SYSTEMS FOR THE RASPBERRY PI

There are many different operating systems available for the Raspberry Pi—too many to list them all. They all have different strengths, depending on what default software they come with and what they are intended for. Some are meant for computer work in general, while others have a more specialized purpose. Many of them are based on Linux, albeit in different flavors. Other examples, aside from Raspbian, are Pidora (based on the Linux distro Fedora) and Arch Linux ARM.

A bit of a special case is Android. It is also based on the Linux-Kernel, but it is more widely known because it is used as the operating system for many mobile devices, like smartphones. That means there are lots of apps available for this OS. However, the only version that will run reliably on the Raspberry Pi is Android 2.3, which is fairly old. A project to get Android 4.0 running on the Raspberry Pi has had limited success and is not supported by the Raspberry Pi Foundation.

An example of an operating system designed for a specific use on the Raspberry Pi is RaspBMC, which turns the minicomputer into a dedicated media center.

RISC OS is an example of an operating system that is not based on Linux. It was originally developed in 1987 for computers with the ARM chip architecture, which the Raspberry Pi uses. It is fast but not as nice to look at or as good at media playback as some of the Linux distros.

An OS geared toward advanced users is Plan 9, a successor to UNIX, which was an operating system originally created in 1969. It is intended mainly for research and offers unique features, especially with regard to networked computing. This makes it very different from the other operating systems that users may be familiar with. Therefore, learning how to use Plan 9 can be very challenging.

It is even possible to learn how to develop an operating system from scratch on the Raspberry Pi, but such a project should be reserved for the particularly ambitious.

different operating systems to compare them and see which one best suits your needs. Some users like to have more than one card with different operating systems so that they can quickly adjust their Raspberry Pi for different tasks.

The Raspberry Pi Foundation also offers its New Out Of Box Software (NOOBS) for download, which is recommended for beginners. On first boot, this software offers four different operating systems to be installed. You can later switch between them.

THE MOST POPULAR OPTION: RASPBIAN

The Raspberry Pi Foundation recommends Raspbian for new users. The first time you boot up your Raspberry Pi under Raspbian, a tool called Raspi-config will start automatically. This is necessary to set up the computer, similar to a BIOS (basic input/output system) on regular PCs. Use the up/down cursor keys to select "expad_rootfs" and hit return. This will expand the root partition to fill the SD card. Otherwise the partition will remain restricted to the space the operating system requires, and the remaining space on the SD card will not be used. If the picture you see is centered in the middle of your TV or monitor with a black border around it, select "overscan" and disable it.

Depending on where you are in the world, you may also want to configure your keyboard and change the time zone and the location using the appropriate menu options. You can also change the password (the default setting is "raspberry," with the username being "pi") if you deem it necessary. Finally, you will probably want to change the "boot_behaviour" so that the Raspberry Pi boots straight to the desktop. Otherwise it will boot to a terminal where you can type in commands and not to the graphical user interface (GUI), which is much easier to work with for most people. If you end up in the text-based terminal, you can type in "startx" to get to the GUI called LXDE Window Manager, which is very similar to Windows or OS X.

Raspbian also comes with many software packages ready for use, so you can start working—or playing—right away. It includes a file manager that allows you to browse through the files stored on the Raspberry Pi with a graphical interface and a task manager that provides information about your computer's performance. It includes Leafpad, a simple text editor; GPic View, an image viewer to look at pictures; and LXMusic to play sound files. It also has various tools to adjust the appearance of the graphical user interface and the settings of your computer, monitor, and input devices. There are also two different web browsers, Midori and NetSurf, preinstalled, which you can use to browse the World Wide Web if your Raspberry Pi is connected to the Internet.

If you are connected to the Internet, you have access to many more software packages. The most convenient way to install new software is using the Pi Store, which you can access through the app of the same name. Similar to Apple's App Store or the Google Play Store, the Pi Store offers a variety of apps and games. Some of them cost money, while others are free. For example, the free app LibreOffice is a complete productivity suite comparable to Microsoft Office.

The other option for installing new software is a package manager called apt (for Advanced Packaging Tool), through which you can get access to even more titles than you can through the Pi Store. It is a bit more difficult to use, though, as it does not operate from the GUI but from the command line. That is, you

LibreOffice, a free office suite, is one example of the many free software titles available for the Raspberry Pi. These often work just as well as commercial options.

have to type in commands to get it to work. A guide to how this works can be found at http://elinux.org/Add_software.

Last but not least, Raspbian comes with tools for programming and learning how to program. Scratch is a graphical programming language aimed at children. It allows young people to create their own games through a simple drag-and-drop system, while learning about the core concepts of programming. IDLE is an integrated development environment (IDE) for the programming language Python. It displays the results of each line of code instantly as it is entered, making it easy to spot any mistakes and allowing for fast coding.

When you are done with your Raspberry Pi session, note that switching off the Raspberry Pi by simply unplugging it can result in the operating system getting corrupted and possibly not being able to boot anymore. To prevent this, use the shutdown option in the bottom right corner of the screen (or alternatively, type "sudo shutdown" into the command line) before disconnecting the power cable.

PROGRAMMING ON THE RASPBERRY PI

Programming a computer means nothing other than getting the computer to perform a desired task by following a set of commands. To make the computer understand the instructions you want it to follow, you need a language that both humans and computers can understand—a programming language. A wide variety of programming languages exist, each with its own strengths and weaknesses, but one has a particular connection to the Raspberry Pi.

PI STANDS FOR PYTHON

When the Raspberry Pi was named, the "Pi" part was not primarily meant as a reference to the circular constant so prominent in mathematics, nor was it solely chosen for the play on words in regard to a baked good. As Eben Upton explains in the *Raspberry Pi User Guide*, "Pi" was a mangling of "Python." At the time they named their device, which was still under development, the creators expected that Python was going to be the only programming language available on their platform. (The "Raspberry" part of the name does not have a deeper meaning behind it; it is simply a continuation of the tradition to name computers after fruit, like Apricot, Apple, and BlackBerry.) This expectation did not hold true, as the Raspberry Pi turned out to be more powerful than they envisioned early in the development process. Today, there are several different programming languages available to use on the minicomputer.

Nonetheless, Python is still one of the most popular options. It is a good choice for learning how to program because it has a clear and consistent structure. As a result, the code is relatively easy to read compared to other programming languages. Python is a high-level programming language, which means it is closer to human language than to the computer's machine language, which consists entirely of numbers.

Python was first developed in the late 1980s by Guido van Rossum at the National Research Institute for Mathematics and Computer Science in the Netherlands as a successor to the ABC programming language. It was not actually named after the snake, but after the British sketch comedy series *Monty Python's Flying Circus*. Van Rossum, who has been proclaimed by the Python community as "Benevolent Dictator for Life," was reading the scripts for the show at the time.

Python is available for all major operating systems, and it works as a cross-platform scripting language. You can write your code on another computer running Windows or OS X and copy your program to your Raspberry Pi or vice versa, as long as the program does not make use of specific hardware

Guido van Rossum, author of the Python programming language, continues to oversee the Python development process. He often speaks at gatherings for the Python community.

like the Raspberry Pi's GPIO port, which other computers do not have.

Several versions of Python exist. The latest, Python 3.0, was released in December 2008. It includes features that were not available in earlier versions of Python, but it is not backward compatible. This means that code written with Python 2.x does not work with Python 3.x without adjusting it. If you are just starting out and don't have any preexisting code, this will not affect you, but it is worth keeping in mind that this disparity between different versions of Python exists. If you

>> SCRATCH

The default distribution of Raspbian comes with another option to learn how to create computer programs, the educational programming language Scratch.

The Lifelong Kindergarten group, located within the Media Lab of the Massachusetts Institute of Technology, has the mission to help "learners of all ages continue to learn through a process of designing, creating, experimenting, and exploring," as children do in kindergarten. This group started the Scratch project in January 2003, and it was released to the public in 2007. A new version—Scratch 2.0—was released in 2013. It is available free of charge, and the source code is available for download.

Whereas with other programming languages you have to type in instructions, Scratch has a graphical user interface that can be navigated with a mouse. By dragging and dropping blocks of instructions and combining them, you can create interactive games and animated stories and share them on the Internet. Millions of projects can be found on the Scratch website (http://scratch.mit.edu).

While on the surface this looks fairly simple and childlike, the idea behind Scratch is that users will learn to think creatively to solve problems and design their programs systematically, just as they would while using any other programming language. In a playful way, Scratch teaches the core concepts of coding without the fairly steep learning curve of text-based programming languages. Users do not have to memorize instructions. They can start creating their own programs right away and see results instantly. Although it is aimed at younger children of ages eight and above, this makes Scratch an interesting starting point for older users wishing to acquaint themselves with the principles of programming.

Since the Raspberry Pi was developed to help people learn how computers and programming work, Scratch seems to be an optimal companion for the minicomputer.

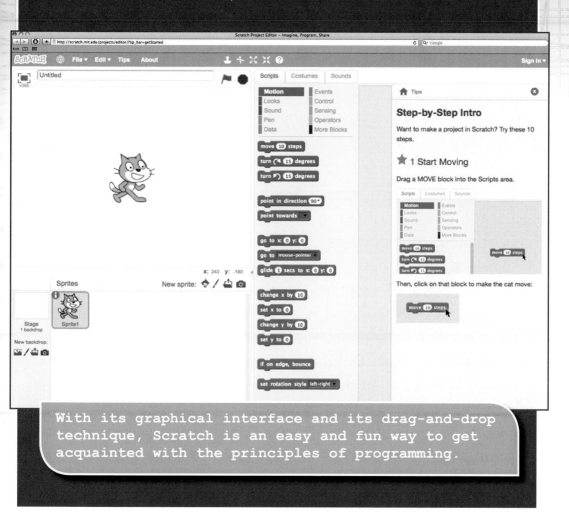

With its graphical interface and its drag-and-drop technique, Scratch is an easy and fun way to get acquainted with the principles of programming.

are looking at code examples in books or on the Internet, you should always check to see if they were intended for the same version of Python you are using to avoid unpleasant surprises.

You can write Python code in a simple text file, using a text editor like Leafpad. A more comfortable way is to use an integrated development environment (IDE), which instantly displays the results of each line of code. Otherwise you have to save your text file and run the program you have written to see if it works the way you intended. The integrated development environment for Python is called IDLE (or IDLE 3 for Python 3.x). Another helpful feature of IDLE is syntax highlighting. It displays different parts of the Python syntax in different colors according to their function, making the code clearer and typing errors easier to spot.

RASPBERRY PI GREETS THE WORLD OF PROGRAMMING

For almost four decades, traditionally one of the first things someone setting out to learn programming will get to know is the "Hello World" program, which outputs the message "Hello, World!" on the display. It is an easy way to illustrate the most basic workings of a programming language.

When you start IDLE, you will see three greater-than signs (>>>). This is called the prompt, which is where you enter the code. When you see it, it means IDLE is ready to accept commands. To create the "Hello World" program, you simply enter "print ("Hello, World!")," and IDLE will display the message. This program may not be particularly exciting, but it shows in a simple manner how you can get a computer to do what you want through programming. Of course it is only the beginning, as Python can be used to create anything from a simple calculator to complex programs and games.

Raspbian comes with a collection of modules for Python called Pygame. Originally written by Pete Shinners, it was designed for creating games in Python by providing functions such as sound and graphics. While it would be possible to create these yourself, it is easier to use already existing options. The development of Pygame continues as a community effort. Information about projects and the regularly held

Students attend a game design course focusing on Pygame. Python and Pygame are good starting points for entering the world of programming.

Python Game Programming Challenge can be found at http://www.pygame.org.

Since Python can make use of the Raspberry Pi's GPIO port, you can use it to write programs that communicate with external hardware, such as sensors, connected to the board.

As mentioned above, Python is not the only programming language that can be used on the Raspberry Pi. Languages include C, C++, Erlang, Java, Perl, PHP, Ruby, and many more. However, it is probably a good idea to concentrate on one language at first to get to know the basic principles of programming before moving on to another.

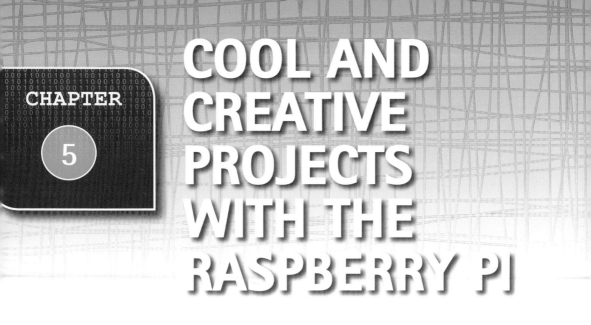

COOL AND CREATIVE PROJECTS WITH THE RASPBERRY PI

Learning how to program is in itself an impressive task and a worthwhile undertaking, but there is a lot more you can do with the Raspberry Pi. Since it was first released, users have come up with creative and unexpected ways to use the minicomputer.

A VERSATILE DEVICE: THE RASPBERRY PI IN ENTERTAINMENT AND SCIENCE

One popular use for the Raspberry Pi is to turn it into a low-cost media center. This is perhaps unsurprising. The SoC used by the Raspberry Pi, the Broadcom BCM2835, was originally developed for home theater PCs (HTPCs) and is capable of decoding and playing full HD 1080p H.264 video. The board was designed to be connected to a TV. There exists software support in the form

If set up correctly, the Raspberry Pi can function as the heart of a media center.

of RaspBMC, a version of the media player XMBC. RaspBMC has been optimized as an operating system for Raspberry Pis used as dedicated HTPCs. It can be downloaded for free from the website of the Raspberry Pi Foundation or from http://www.raspbmc.com.

The Raspberry Pi can be used to play videos and music files that are stored locally—usually on an external hard disk drive or another storage device—or to stream them from the Internet. RaspBMC offers an intuitive graphical user interface, which can be controlled via keyboard and mouse. A wireless remote control with a receiver that is connected to the Raspberry Pi via USB is an elegant and inexpensive alternative to save the space the input devices would normally take up. The board itself is small enough to hide behind the TV screen, making your low-budget media center all but invisible.

The Raspberry Pi is great for another form of entertainment, too. While it may not run the latest games, the relatively low computing power is not a problem if you want to use your Raspberry Pi for retro gaming. The minicomputer can handle games from the dawn of computer gaming in the 1970s up to roughly the year 2000. These classics may not look as flashy as current games, but they still offer lots of fun and for many older Pi enthusiasts, a hefty dose of nostalgia. There are plenty of emulators available to make these old games run on the Raspberry Pi. People have completed projects that have used the minicomputer as the heart of an arcade machine (an example of such a device can be seen at www.raspberrypi.org/archives/2412). People have also converted old gaming consoles like the Nintendo Entertainment System or the Gameboy into a case for the Pi to make it fit aesthetically with their intended purpose. Using the Raspberry Pi for retro gaming is so popular that Picade, a kit to build your own retro arcade machine, was funded on Kickstarter in late 2012. Similar to RaspBMC, which turns the minicomputer into a dedicated media center, there is also an operating system called RetroPi, which turns it into a dedicated gaming machine.

Although the computing power of the Raspberry Pi is relatively low, the small board has even been used to create supercomputers, in which a large number of processors are linked together to work on the same problem. A team of computer engineers at the University of Southampton led by Professor Simon Cox used sixty-four Raspberry Pis to make a supercomputer named

Professor Simon Cox built a supercomputer out of Raspberry Pis. He enlisted his son James to build the case out of LEGOs.

Iridis-Pi (after Iridis, the university's large supercomputer), complete with a case made from LEGOs, designed by Professor Cox's six-year-old son. While the result is not particularly powerful as far as supercomputers go, it is enough to demonstrate the principles of supercomputing for a relatively low price. Joshua Kiepert, a student at Boise State University, built a similar cluster out of thirty-three overclocked Raspberry Pis to help him with the work on his dissertation. By doing this, he made himself independent in his research from the university's supercomputer, to which he did not always have access. Videos of and building instructions for both of these machines can be found online.

>> WHIPPED CREAM ON YOUR PI: OPTIONAL ENHANCEMENTS

The Raspberry Pi on its own can be used for many things, but there are inexpensive optional enhancements available that open up even more possibilities. These are called breakout boards or prototyping boards, and they make it easier to connect other devices to the Raspberry Pi.

The Fen Logic Gertboard is an add-on board for the minicomputer to expand the use of its GPIO pins and connect it to the outside

Add-ons like the Gertboard increase the capabilities of the Raspberry Pi.

world by sending and receiving signals. It can be used to control lights, switches, sensors, motors, and more. For anyone interested in robotics and physical computing, this is a very appealing option. The Gertboard was named after its creator, Gert van Loo, who was involved in the design of the Raspberry Pi's SoC processor. Originally the Gertboard came unassembled and you had to solder it yourself, but there are assembled Gertboards available now.

A similar, but not quite as versatile, device is the PiFace Digital. Unlike the bigger Gertboard, it is the same size as the Raspberry Pi and sits right on top of it when you connect it to the GPIO pins, making a neat little package. This may give it an edge over the Gertboard if available space is a concern for your project.

There are also other options available, such as the Ciseco Slice of Pi, the HumblePi, or the Adafruit Prototyping Pi Plate, and it is possible to build your own custom circuit board, too. Another possible enhancement is the Arduino, a microcontroller for physical computing first created in 2005. Unlike the devices previously mentioned, the Arduino was not developed specifically for the Raspberry Pi, but it is often used with it.

WHERE NO PI HAS GONE BEFORE

Due to its diminutive size and low power requirements, the Raspberry Pi is not restricted to being used at home or in a lab. There have been attempts to combine a battery-powered Pi with video glasses to turn it into a wearable computer, similar to the highly anticipated Google Glass, although admittedly not quite as slick.

Rapiro, a robot designed by Shota Ishiwatari, has a Raspberry Pi in its head that serves as a programmable brain.

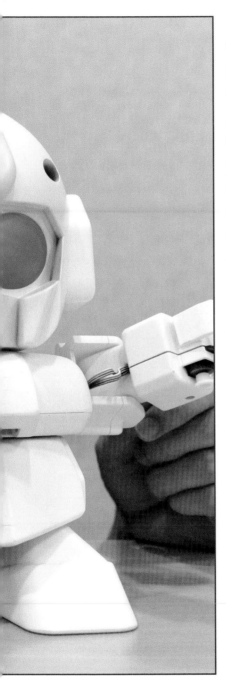

Raspberry Pis can also be set up as web servers, Internet radios, audiobook readers, home automation servers, and car computers that serve as media players and GPS units—the possibilities seem endless. And that is before you take into consideration that the Raspberry Pi can also be used for physical computing and robotics, especially with the use of extension boards like the Gertboard or PiFace.

A relatively simple project to show how the Raspberry Pi can respond to the analog world and a nice idea for Halloween is Gordon Henderson's Pumpkin Pi. In an article in *The MagPi*, Henderson gives instructions on how to equip a pumpkin with LED eyes and a motion detector and use the Raspberry Pi to control them so that the pumpkin's eyes flicker when the sensor detects movement. Scary sounds can be added for additional effect.

If you think your Raspberry Pi needs more vegetables, take a look at the BeetBox (http://scott.j38.net/interactive/beetbox). This musical instrument, created by designer Scott Garner, plays drumbeats when the player touches actual beets set into a hardwood enclosure. The touch sensor is connected to a Raspberry Pi, which plays the triggered drum samples.

Similarly eccentric, although in a different way, is Greg Holloway's project Fish Pi, which aims to develop an autonomous marine surface vehicle. A Raspberry Pi, protected from the elements by an upside-down lunch box, is planned to control an unmanned vessel powered by a solar panel. This vessel is supposed to navigate autonomously on—and eventually cross—the Atlantic Ocean and take environmental measurements for educational purposes. You can follow this project at http://fishpi.org.

Dave Akerman (http://www.daveakerman.com) has taken the Raspberry Pi in another direction: up. In his project, called Raspberry Pi in the Sky, he has incorporated the minicomputer into his hobby of high-altitude ballooning. He has used weather balloons to take Raspberry Pis equipped with a camera module—and protected by creative casings like a raspberry made from foam material or a teddy bear—25 miles (40 kilometers) up into the atmosphere. They are then dropped and fall down to earth in a parachute, taking a video of the decline. With this project, Akerman holds the record for the highest pictures transmitted in real time from an amateur device.

But the Raspberry Pi has even higher aspirations and will not stop at the edge of space. In an interview with Nick Heath of TechRepublic.com, Eben Upton said that he could see Raspberry Pis being used in satellites as a cheap alternative to the traditionally customized, and therefore expensive, computer platforms. One user of the Raspberry Pi Foundation's forum claimed in

This ornamental model of a Bavarian house is equipped with a Raspberry Pi, which acts as a security camera.

April 2013 that he would send a Raspberry Pi, equipped with pressure and temperature sensors, into low orbit on a satellite for educational purposes, but so far the claim remains unconfirmed. Nonetheless, it seems only a matter of time before the Raspberry Pi crosses this final frontier.

For the Raspberry Pi, it appears, not even the sky is the limit. Creative minds come up with new projects for it every day. Some of them are practical, some rather kooky, but all offer an entertaining way to learn about computers and electronics. The end of the Raspberry Pi's success story is not in sight, and there are bound to be many exciting developments yet.

ARM Short for Advanced RISC Machine, it is a microprocessor based on a reduced instruction set computer (RISC) architecture, first developed by Acorn Computers in the 1980s.

CENTRAL PROCESSING UNIT (CPU) The element of a computer system that processes all the instructions that let the computer perform tasks.

COMPOSITE VIDEO A video out port for which almost all TVs have a corresponding input. It has poorer resolution than HDMI.

DISTRO Short for distribution, it is a specific version of Linux, such as Debian or Fedora.

GNU Short for GNU's Not UNIX, it is a UNIX-like operating system developed by the GNU Project, which propagates free software.

GPIO Short for general purpose input/output, it is a programmable port that can be used to connect external hardware.

GRAPHICAL USER INTERFACE (GUI) A program interface that allows the user to interact with a computer through graphical icons, rather than text-based commands.

GRAPHICS PROCESSING UNIT (GPU) The chip that handles a computer's graphics.

HDMI Short for high-definition multimedia interface, a digital interface that transmits both audio and video data.

INTEGRATED DEVELOPMENT ENVIRONMENT (IDE) A programming environment that provides tools such as a GUI builder, text or code editor, and debugger. It makes programming more user-friendly by making it easier to test the entered code and spot mistakes.

LINUX A free operating system, first created by Linus Torvalds in 1991, that is available in many different versions, also known as distros.

MEDIA CENTER A computer connected to a TV that allows audio and video playback and recording.

OPERATING SYSTEM (OS) A collection of software that interacts with the hardware and allows other software to run.

OVERCLOCK To make a computer or component run faster than the speed for which it has been tested and approved.

PHYSICAL COMPUTING The use of hardware and software to build systems that can sense and respond to input from the real world.

PYTHON A programming language developed by Guido van Rossum that gave the Raspberry Pi part of its name.

RAM Short for random access memory, it is a type of computer memory that temporarily stores data that is currently in use and allows it to be accessed directly in any random order.

RASPBIAN An operating system based on the Linux distro Debian that has been optimized for the Raspberry Pi.

RASPBMC An operating system for the Raspberry Pi that turns it into a media center.

SD CARD Short for secure digital card, it is a form of flash memory that the Raspberry Pi uses to store data.

SOC Short for system-on-chip, it is a chip that integrates all the necessary components of a computer.

USB Short for universal serial bus, it is a standardized connection for computer peripherals such as keyboards.

Adafruit Industries
150 Varick Street
New York, NY 10013
Web Site: http://learn.adafruit.com/category/raspberry-pi
Adafruit was started as a company to produce and sell electronics and to help people learn how to use them and make
things themselves. It offers dozens of tutorials for projects
with the Raspberry Pi.

Allied Electronics
7151 Jack Newell Boulevard South
Fort Worth, TX 76118
(866) 433-5722
Website: http://www.alliedelec.com
Allied Electronics is the distributing partner of the Raspberry Pi
Foundation in North America.

CodeNow
920 U Street NW
Washington, DC 20001
(202) 555-1212
Website: http://codenow.org
The mission of this nonprofit organization is to teach underrepre-
sented youth the foundational skills of computer
programming. It provides free out-of-school training in
computer programming, hosted at local tech companies.

Code.org
P.O. Box 34628 #80740
Seattle, WA 98124-1628
(931) 996-2633
Website: http://www.code.org
Code.org, a nonprofit organization funded by high-tech legends
such as Bill Gates and Mark Zuckerberg, is dedicated to
growing computer science education worldwide.

IEEE Computer Society
2001 L Street NW, Suite 700
Washington, DC 20036-4928
(202) 371-0101
Website: http://www.computer.org
The Computer Society of the Institute of Electrical and Electronics
Engineers, which traces its origins back to 1946, aims to
further the knowledge of computer science and technology.
To that end, it offers up-to-date information and training.

Make Magazine
Maker Media Inc.
1005 Gravenstein Highway North
Sebastopol, CA 95472
Website: http://makezine.com/category/electronics/
raspberry-pi
Maker Media is a leader in the worldwide "maker movement,"
and its *Make* magazine covers many different topics related

to the movement's do-it-yourself credo, including numerous articles on the Raspberry Pi.

The Raspberry Pi Foundation
Mitchell Wood House
Caldecote CB23 7NU
England
011 44 07831161534
Website: http://www.raspberrypi.org
This is the England-based charity that developed the Raspberry Pi. Its website offers software downloads and a highly frequented forum.

WEBSITES

Due to the changing nature of Internet links, Rosen Publishing has developed an online list of websites related to the subject of this book. This site is updated regularly. Please use this link to access the list:

http://www.rosenlinks.com/CODE/Rasp

Blum, Richard, and Christine Bresnahan. *SAMS Teach Yourself Python Programming for Raspberry Pi in 24 Hours.* Indianapolis, IN: SAMS Publishing, 2013.

Dennis, Andrew. *Raspberry Pi Home Automation with Arduino.* Birmingham, England: Packt Publishing, 2013.

Girling, Gray. *Raspberry Pi Manual: A Practical Guide to the Revolutionary Small Computer.* Sparkford, England: Haynes, 2013.

Golden, Rick. *Raspberry Pi Networking Cookbook.* Birmingham, England: Packt Publishing, 2013.

Goodwin, Steven. *Smart Home Automation with Linux and Raspberry Pi.* Berkeley, CA: Apress, 2013.

Horan, Brendan. *Practical Raspberry Pi.* New York, NY: Apress, 2013.

McGrath, Mike. *Raspberry Pi in Easy Steps.* Warwickshire, England: In Easy Steps, 2013.

Membrey, Peter, and David Hows. *Learn Raspberry Pi with Linux.* New York, NY: Apress, 2012.

Monk, Simon. *Programming the Raspberry Pi: Getting Started with Python.* New York, NY: McGraw-Hill, 2013.

Narzako, Sam. *Raspberry Pi Media Center: Transform Your Raspberry Pi into a Full-Blown Media Center Within 24 Hours.* Birmingham, England: Packt Publishing, 2013.

Norris, Donald. *Raspberry Pi Projects for the Evil Genius.* New York, NY: McGraw-Hill, 2013.

Richardson, Matt, and Shawn Wallace. *Getting Started with Raspberry Pi.* Sebastopol, CA: O'Reilly Media, 2012.

Robinson, Andrew, and Mike Cook. *Raspberry Pi Projects.*
Chichester, England: John Wiley & Sons, 2013.

Severance, Charles R., and Kristin Fontichiaro. *Raspberry Pi (Makers as Innovators).* Ann Arbor, MI: Cherry Lake Publishing, 2014.

Smith, Bruce F. *Raspberry Pi Assembly Language: Beginners Hands-on Guide.* North Charleston, SC: CreateSpace Independent Publishing Platform, 2013.

Sogelid, Stefan. *Raspberry Pi for Secret Agents.* Birmingham, England: Packt Publishing, 2013.

Suehle, Ruth, and Tom Callaway. *Raspberry Pi Hacks: Tips and Tools for Making Things with the Inexpensive Linux Computer.* Sebastopol, CA: O'Reilly Media, 2013.

Upton, Eben, and Gareth Halfacree. *Raspberry Pi User Guide.* Chichester, England: John Wiley & Sons, 2012.

Warner, Timothy. *Hacking Raspberry Pi.* Indianapolis, IN: Que Publishing, 2013.

Wentk, Richard. *Raspberry Pi (Teach Yourself Visually).* Indianapolis, IN: John Wiley & Sons, 2013.

Akerman, Dave. "PIE1—Raspberry Pi Sends Live Images from Near Space." July 16, 2012. Retrieved November 18, 2013 (http://www.daveakerman.com/?p=592).

Bartmann, Erik. *Durchstarten mit Raspberry Pi.* Köln, Germany: O'Reilly Verlag, 2012.

Bort, Julie. "10 Mind-Blowing Raspberry Pi Projects." *Business Insider*, January 13, 2013. Retrieved November 18, 2013 (http://www.businessinsider.com/10-mind-blowing-raspberry -pi-projects-2013-1).

Cawley, Christian. *Great Things, Small Package: Your Unofficial Raspberry Pi Manual.* Essex, England: MakeUseOf, 2013. Kindle ed.

Computing at School. *Raspberry Pi Education Manual, Version 1.0.* December 2012. Retrieved May 31, 2013 (http://downloads .raspberrypi.org/Raspberry_Pi_Education_Manual.pdf).

Free Software Foundation. "Philosophy of the GNU Project." Retrieved November 18, 2013 (http://www.gnu.org/ philosophy/philosophy.en.html).

Hayward, David. "Raspberry Pi Operating Systems: 5 Reviewed and Rated." TechRadar.com, May 9, 2013. Retrieved November 18, 2013 (http://www.techradar.com/news/ software/operating-systems/raspberry-pi-operating-systems -5-reviewed-and-rated-1147941).

Heath, Nick. "Raspberry Pi: How a $25 Computer Could Spark a Computing Revolution." *TechRepublic*, February 8, 2012. Retrieved November 18, 2013 (http://www.techrepublic .com/blog/european-technology/raspberry-pi-how-a -25-computer-could-spark-a-computing-revolution/123).

Henderson, Gordon. "Pumpkin Pi." *The MagPi*, October 2012. Retrieved November 18, 2013 (http://www.themagpi.com/issue/issue-6/pdf).

Holloway, Greg. "Fish Pi." June 26, 2012. Retrieved November 18, 2013 (http://www.raspberrypi.org/archives/1479).

Kiepert, Joshua. "Creating a Raspberry Pi-Based Beowulf Cluster." *Boise State University*, May 22, 2013. Retrieved November 18, 2013 (http://coen.boisestate.edu/ece/files/2013/05/Creating.a.Raspberry.Pi-Based.Beowulf.Cluster_v2.pdf).

McManus, Sean, and Mike Cook. *Raspberry Pi for Dummies.* Hoboken, NJ: John Wiley & Sons, 2013.

Plafke, James. "The True Cost of a Raspberry Pi Is More Than You Think." *ExtremeTech*, February 15, 2013. Retrieved November 18, 2013 (http://www.extremetech.com/computing/148482-the-true-cost-of-a-raspberry-pi-is-more-than-you-think).

Python Software Foundation. "General Python FAQ—Python v2.7.6 Documentation." 2013. Retrieved November 18, 2013 (http://docs.python.org/2/faq/general.html).

Raspberry Pi Foundation. "About Us." Retrieved November 18, 2013 (http://www.raspberrypi.org/about).

Scratch. "About Scratch." Retrieved November 18, 2013 (http://scratch.mit.edu/about).

Steventon, Jacques. "Sending the Pi to Space (Pi Satellite)." April 18, 2013. Retrieved November 18, 2013 (www.raspberrypi.org/phpBB3/viewtopic.php?t=41030).

Treacy, Megan. "20 Awesome Projects for Raspberry Pi Microcomputers." TreeHugger, February 5, 2013. Retrieved

November 18, 2013 (http://www.treehugger.com/slideshows/gadgets/20-awesome-projects-raspberry-pi-microcomputers).

University of Southampton. "Steps to Make a Raspberry Pi Supercomputer." October 2013. Retrieved November 18, 2013 (http://www.southampton.ac.uk/~sjc/raspberrypi).

Upton, Eben, and Gareth Halfacree. *Raspberry Pi: Einstieg und User Guide*. Heidelberg, Germany: mitp, 2013.

Watson, Alison. *The Big Book of Raspberry Pi*. North Charleston, SC: CreateSpace Independent Publishing Platform, 2013. Kindle ed.

ABOUT THE AUTHOR

Dr. Nicki Peter Petrikowski is a literary scholar as well as an editor, author, and translator. Having grown up in the 1980s, he fondly remembers many an hour spent in front of the home computers of that time.

PHOTO CREDITS

Designer: Nicole Russo; Editor: Andrea Sclarow Paskoff; Photo Researcher: Amy Feinberg

24.70

WITHDRAWN